W9-AXA-941

Owi

THE NEWTOWN
SCHOOL
SHOOTING

THE NEWTOWN
SCHOOL
SHOOTING

BY LISA OWINGS

CONTENT CONSULTANT
JACLYN SCHILDKRAUT
DOCTORAL CANDIDATE
SCHOOL OF CRIMINAL JUSTICE
TEXAS STATE UNIVERSITY

ABDO
Publishing Company

CREDITS

Published by ABDO Publishing Company, PO Box 398166, Minneapolis, MN 55439. Copyright © 2014 by Abdo Consulting Group, Inc. International copyrights reserved in all countries. No part of this book may be reproduced in any form without written permission from the publisher. The Essential Library™ is a trademark and logo of ABDO Publishing Company.

Printed in the United States of America,
North Mankato, Minnesota
082013
012014

 THIS BOOK CONTAINS AT LEAST 10% RECYCLED MATERIALS.

Editor: Melissa York
Series Designer: Becky Daum

Photo credits: Shannon Hicks, Newtown Bee/AP Images, cover, 2, 33, 39; Google/AP Images, 6; Jessica Hill/AP Images, 10, 26, 65, 78, 82, 86, 91, 95; Rex USA, 12 (left), 21, 25; Eastern Connecticut University/AP Images, 12 (right); Western Connecticut State University/AP Images, 14; AP Images, 21, 67; Eliza Hallabeck, Newtown Bee/AP Images, 29; Melanie Stengel, The New Haven Register/AP Images, 40; Andrew Gombert/AP Images, 47; Charles Krupa/AP Images, 50; Seth Wenig/AP Images, 52; Susan Walsh/AP Images, 55; The Courier, Kirk Sides/AP Images, 58; Craig Ruttle/AP Images, 61; NBC News/AP Images, 62; Journal Inquirer, Jared Ramsdell/AP Images, 70, 74

Library of Congress Control Number: 2013941146

Cataloging-in-Publication Data

Owings, Lisa.
The Newtown School shooting / Lisa Owings.
    p. cm. -- (Essential events)
ISBN 978-1-62403-055-0
Includes bibliographical references and index.
1. Sandy Hook Elementary shooting, Newtown, Connecticut, 2012--Juvenile literature.
2. School shootings--Connecticut--Newtown--Juvenile literature. I. Title.
364--dc23

                                                              2013941146

CONTENTS

CHAPTER
ONE

LOCKDOWN

It was less than two weeks until Christmas. The staff at Sandy Hook Elementary School in Newtown, Connecticut, drove past quiet houses festooned with wreaths and lights on their way to work the morning of Friday, December 14, 2012. When they arrived at the school, they made their way to their classrooms and offices.

On the bus, children in kindergarten through fourth grade chatted with their classmates until they pulled up in front of Sandy Hook just before 9:00 a.m. Then they hopped off the buses, and teachers shepherded them into the school. The kindergarten and first-grade classrooms were just inside the front doors. The older children walked farther down the halls to their classrooms.

As classes started throughout Sandy Hook Elementary School, teachers took attendance and waited for their young students to settle into their desks. Loudspeakers crackled to life, and children across the school listened to morning announcements. They put

Sandy Hook Elementary School was calm the morning of December 14, 2012.

their hands over their hearts as they recited the Pledge of Allegiance.

While these daily activities got under way, Principal Dawn Hochsprung sat down with school psychologist Mary Sherlach, lead teacher Natalie Hammond, and other staff in a meeting about one of the school's second-grade students.

An Interrupted Meeting

At 9:30, due to a recently updated security system, the school doors locked. Anyone arriving after 9:30 normally had to be buzzed in. Around the same time, Principal Hochsprung and the other staff in the conference room heard a strange popping sound and shattering glass. Hochsprung, Sherlach, and Hammond rushed into the hallway to find out what was going on. None of them expected to encounter a man armed with a semiautomatic rifle who was obviously intending to use it.

Hochsprung warned the women behind her to stay back and lock the conference room door. Then she lunged toward the shooter in an attempt to stop him.

Amid sprays of gunfire and shouts of "Shooter, stay put!" Hammond dashed back toward the relative safety of the conference room.[1] Hochsprung and Sherlach were no longer with her. Hammond closed the door behind her and, because it didn't have a lock, she used her body to hold it shut. She was shot multiple times, but she survived and likely saved the lives of everyone else in the room.

Panic Spreads

The sounds of rapid gunfire filled the school's hallways. Those near enough to hear it knew immediately something was wrong. Even in their panic, they found ways to warn those farther from the shooting they were in danger.

Someone in the front office managed to switch on the intercom. Teachers and students in every Sandy Hook classroom listened in shock and horror as gunshots, screams, and desperate cries streamed from the loudspeakers. The teachers knew then their lives and the lives of their students were at

LETHAL WEAPONS

Investigators found the shooter inside the school armed with a semiautomatic Bushmaster rifle loaded with a 30-round magazine. He also carried two semiautomatic handguns; one was made by Glock, the other by Sig Sauer. The shooter used the Bushmaster rifle in his rampage, firing off 154 shots in less than five minutes.[2]

Natalie Hammond later received recognition for her bravery during the shooting.

risk. They jumped into action, doing whatever they could to keep the children safe. Doors were locked and barricaded, windows were covered, and children were comforted, tucked into hiding places, and told to keep quiet, just as they would be during a lockdown drill.

As the shooting continued, custodian Rick Thorne rushed through the halls issuing urgent warnings to anyone who had not realized what was happening. As he passed each classroom, he locked any door left open.

Instead of heading for safety, Thorne remained in the hallway and stood guard outside the locked classrooms as the shooter prowled the school.

Teachers Take Action

When second-grade teacher Abbey Clements heard what she thought might be gunshots, she peeked outside the classroom. She noticed two children standing in the hallway outside her door, completely exposed to danger. Clements pulled the children out of the hallway

LOCK THE DOOR

Without custodian Rick Thorne's presence in Sandy Hook hallways, the tragedy could have been even greater. Classroom doors in the school did not lock from the inside. That meant during the shooting teachers had to either barricade their unlocked doors or risk stepping into the hallway to turn the lock. Thorne's instinct to lock all the doors allowed teachers to remain safe inside their classrooms.

After the shooting, reading consultant Becky Virgalla was among those who urged the school to make sure classroom doors could be locked from the inside. She said,

Ours did not and teachers had to go out. You can't be out in a hall when a shooter is present in your school. Just that simple thing could make a difference in time and safety of the children.[3]

Many schools are now considering changing their locks to increase security. Although replacing locks in every classroom is expensive, it is an easy way for teachers to keep their students safer. According to the US Department of Homeland Security, "The capability to quickly lock the door from either side is the fastest solution for 'lockdown' situations."[4]

Lauren Rousseau, *left*, and Victoria Soto, *right*, tried to save their students.

to safety. She locked the door and got her students to a secure place. Then she dialed 911.

Toward the front of the school, kindergarten teacher Janet Vollmer did exactly what she had been trained to do during lockdown drills. She locked the door, covered the windows, and kept her five-year-old students calm by reading them a story. When the kindergartners began getting nervous, Vollmer assured them they would be safe because they were all together.

Not far from Vollmer's classroom, first-grade teacher Kaitlin Roig heard shooting just outside her door. Hers was the first classroom inside the entrance to the school. Roig hurried her students into the bathroom, trying to comfort them as she crowded them into the tiny space. She helped some of them stand on the toilet so they would all fit. She turned off the lights in the room and dragged a bookshelf in front of the bathroom door. Then she slipped inside the bathroom with her students and locked the door behind her.

In two other first-grade classrooms, teachers Lauren Rousseau and Victoria Soto rushed to protect their students. Rousseau guided her students away from the door that would soon open. Soto did the same, trying to hide her students wherever she could. Then she stood bravely between her students and the door she wouldn't have time to lock.

LET ME IN!

Music teacher Maryrose Kristopik had a class of fourth graders in her charge when the shooting broke out. She acted quickly to hide them all in a closet, and she held the door shut from the inside. Kristopik comforted the children by speaking softly to them, hugging them, and holding their hands. Some report that the shooter came as close as the other side of the door, banging on it and yelling, "Let me in!" Parents praised Kristopik as a hero. She acknowledged the bravery of all the staff at the school that day, saying, "I did what any other teacher would have done."[5]

CHAPTER
TWO

A QUIET BOY

T he man with the gun was 20-year-old Adam Lanza. After killing 20 children and six adults at Sandy Hook Elementary School, he turned one of the guns on himself. Police found Lanza's body, clad in black battle fatigues and a military vest, at the door of Soto's classroom.

As the gunman's name blazed across newspapers and television screens, people throughout the country asked themselves the same questions over and over again. *Who was Adam Lanza? What could have driven him to murder innocent children?* No one seemed to have the answers. But in the months after the shooting, news reporters and investigators began uncovering the story of Lanza's short life. They hoped it would offer at least some small key to understanding the incomprehensible tragedy.

Early Days in New Hampshire

Adam Lanza was born on April 22, 1992, in Kingston, New Hampshire. His mother, Nancy Lanza, had grown

No one knows what led Adam Lanza to open fire at Sandy Hook Elementary School.

SENSORY PROCESSING DISORDER

Sensory processing disorder results from a difference in the way a person's brain processes information from the senses. Sensory information becomes jumbled in the brain. Everyday sights, sounds, smells, tastes, and touches are often overwhelming or confusing. Adam Lanza, for example, avoided loud sounds and physical touch.

Without the right sensory information, basic tasks can become challenging. Sensory processing disorder can cause anxiety, depression, behavioral problems, and difficulty in school, among other issues. It is often misdiagnosed. Although most people with sensory processing disorder are not autistic, a large percentage of people with autism have some form of sensory processing disorder.

up there before marrying his father, Peter Lanza, in 1981. Adam also had an older brother, Ryan, born in 1988.

It became apparent early on that Adam had more social difficulties than other kids his age. Adam was noticeably quiet and tended to distance himself from other children. If anyone touched him, he would get angry and upset. According to a family member, Adam was soon diagnosed with sensory processing disorder, a condition that makes everyday sights, sounds, and touches seem overwhelming. Adam's social struggles became more problematic when he started school. Concerned, Nancy worked with school officials to develop an Individual Education Plan (IEP) for her young son.

New Town, New School

In 1998, Peter Lanza was offered a high-paying job in Connecticut, and the Lanzas soon settled into a luxurious home in Newtown. Nancy had heard good things about the schools in the area. She was excited to enroll Adam, then six years old, at Sandy Hook Elementary School. She hoped he would have an easier time there than he had at his school in New Hampshire.

In some ways, he did. Adam seemed to thrive at Sandy Hook. He made lots of new friends and even participated in school plays. But the underlying issues were still there. Adam was still shy and quiet. He rarely ventured out of his own world to connect with other kids. Nancy began questioning whether the public school system could offer her son the special attention he needed. She enrolled him in a program that allowed him to do most of his learning at home. Whatever schoolwork Adam was unable to do there, he was allowed to complete at the school after the other children had gone home.

Around this time, the Lanzas' marriage began crumbling. Nancy complained to friends her husband was spending too much time at work. By 2001, things had reached a breaking point. Although his financial support never ceased, Peter moved out of the family home. He came back to visit his sons frequently.

Middle School Struggles

After Adam had some time to adjust to his father being out of the house, Nancy thought her son might be ready to try mainstream schooling again. Adam attended seventh grade at Newtown's public middle school. But middle school meant moving between classrooms and navigating noisy, crowded hallways. It was too much for Adam. Nancy thought a private school with fewer students would be a more suitable environment for her son. So she moved Adam to Saint Rose of Lima, another Newtown school, for eighth grade.

It was during middle school Adam was diagnosed with Asperger's syndrome, a form of autism, as a family member told reporters after the shooting. People with Asperger's syndrome, although usually highly intelligent, have difficulty with social skills. Adam continued struggling at Saint Rose of Lima despite the smaller class sizes and individual attention. Unsure where else to turn, Nancy pulled her son out of Saint Rose before he finished the school year.

Hope in High School

Adam's older brother left home for college in 2006. The same year, Adam reappeared at Newtown's public high school. There, he had the added support of a special-education program designed for students with social challenges. While other students chatted with friends or strode briskly through the halls to class, Adam could be seen pressed against the wall, avoiding the glances of other students and clutching the briefcase he always carried.

The school district's head of security, Richard Novia, worried Adam was at risk of being bullied. Novia also served as adviser to the school's Technology Club. Since Adam seemed to have an interest in

ASPERGER'S SYNDROME

People with Asperger's syndrome have difficulty interacting with people and reading social cues. For example, they might have trouble understanding when someone is being sarcastic or making a joke. They also tend to engage in repetitive behaviors and avoid eye contact. However, people with Asperger's generally have good language skills and are highly intelligent. Many show extreme interest in a narrow range of topics.

It is common for people with Asperger's to become upset over even minor changes in routine. Children with the condition often get angry or throw tantrums in response to such changes, but there is no evidence Asperger's syndrome causes violent behavior. With support and therapy, many people with Asperger's grow into high-functioning adults.

computers, Novia suggested to Nancy her son might benefit from joining the Technology Club. Novia promised to help guide Adam's interactions with the other kids. Nancy reluctantly agreed.

Under Novia's careful attention, Adam gradually came to tolerate close interaction with Novia and other members of the club. He even posed with the group for a yearbook picture. He got good grades, and a family member noted he was studying Mandarin Chinese and learning to play the saxophone.

Novia continued working with Adam throughout his freshman and sophomore years. Though Adam's social

TECHNOLOGY CLUB

The Technology Club at Newtown High School was responsible for filming school events including sports and graduations, which the students aired on a local cable channel. Other club activities included building and programming robots and computers.

Club adviser Richard Novia knew about Adam's challenges and did everything he could to help the teen overcome them. He told the *Hartford Courant,*

I'd go up and sit next to him. If he was sitting on the floor in the corner somewhere, I would do the same. . . . If it took a half an hour to sit there in silence with him, at some point, you'd go, "How we doing?" And you wouldn't get an answer. . . . But I had a gadget [similar to a Palm Pilot] with me at one time, where I handed him the gadget, and . . . at some point, he started to play with it. And that actually . . . got him to start to come back and interact.[1]

Adam posed with the Technology Club in
Newtown High School's yearbook.

skills were constantly improving, there were frequent
setbacks. Typical of people with Asperger's, Adam
did not respond well to changes in his environment or
routine. According to Novia, his response would be to
completely shut down, drawing into himself. Another
way Adam escaped social pressures was by playing video
games. As reported in the media after the shooting,

Novia recalled in an interview that Adam showed particular interest in violent games such as *World of Warcraft*. But so did plenty of other high school kids. Only years later would the media cast Adam's enjoyment of these games in a potentially disturbing light.

> "It's not like people picked on [Adam] for [his social awkwardness]. From what I saw, people just let him be, and that was that."[2]
> —Matt Baier, a former classmate of Adam's

More Changes

In 2008, Novia left the Newtown school district and moved to Tennessee. Adam would not be returning to the high school either. That summer of 2008, after his sophomore year, 16-year-old Adam enrolled in several classes at Western Connecticut State University. His social isolation was magnified by the fact that he was years younger than most college students. Even so, he managed to get good grades. Nancy hoped this was a step toward independence for Adam. However, he didn't continue with classes beyond that year.

Late in 2008, after several years of separation, Nancy filed for divorce. The process stretched into 2009, and the divorce was finalized in September. After, Adam continued living with his mother. Peter spent time with his sons each week as usual.

The Years before Newtown

In 2010, Adam made a brief appearance at Norwalk Community College before dropping out of school altogether. He also cut off contact with his father and brother that year, severing all social ties except with his mother. No one is sure why.

Concerned about her son's dependence on her, Nancy did her best to teach Adam—then 18 years old—how to be a responsible and self-sufficient adult. She taught him to drive, and Adam received his license in 2010. He also landed a part-time job at a computer shop in town. During Nancy's fairly frequent travels, she would leave Adam at home, giving him a taste of what it would be like for him to live on his own.

One activity the two of them enjoyed together was target shooting. Nancy owned a number of guns, and she periodically took Adam to the shooting range with her. She spoke enthusiastically to friends about her gun collection and love of shooting. It was an opportunity for Nancy to bond with her son and share a favorite hobby.

PARENTING MISTAKES?

Novia suggested Adam's mother made at least two grave mistakes that may have contributed to the Sandy Hook tragedy. One was pulling him out of Newtown High School, where he had developed several support networks. Novia stated:

> Suddenly, when she pulls him out of there, he loses . . . the tech club team he was involved in. He loses friends that he had made. . . . He loses his special ed, he loses his school psychologist, he loses the devoted school administrators.[3]

The other mistake was exposing Adam to guns. According to Novia, "If you have a child . . . with mental disorders or learning disabilities, to have involved him with guns in the first place would be bad."[4] He believes this exposure cost Nancy her life.

Nancy always seemed positive and upbeat around her friends. She never hinted her struggles with Adam had escalated. There was only her wish for her son to have a normal life. Still, some of her close friends began suspecting something might be amiss. Longtime friend Marvin LaFontaine had noticed Nancy wasn't making much of an effort to keep in touch anymore. When LaFontaine spoke to Nancy's brother in 2011 or 2012, he learned Nancy was not speaking to him either. It struck him as odd that Nancy would cut herself off from her family.

Adding to the air of concern was Nancy's apparent plan to move with Adam away from her New England friends and family. She had been trying to find the

Nancy was growing increasingly isolated from friends and family in the months leading up to the shooting.

perfect fit for her 20-year-old son to finish college, and toward the end of 2012, it seemed as if she had found it, either across the country in Washington or in North Carolina. It is unclear whether Adam was on board with his mother's plan.

CHAPTER
THREE

NEWTOWN CHANGES FOREVER

History may never know what was going through Adam Lanza's head in the months leading up to the shooting. If he had been obsessively researching and planning his attack, or if he had hinted at a reason for his desire to kill, he likely destroyed the evidence by smashing one of his hard drives. We do know that by December 14, 2012, Lanza was ready to take violent action.

That morning, Lanza awoke to the familiar surroundings of his home on Yogananda Street. His mother was still sleeping. Lanza went to the place where she kept her guns. He picked up a .22 caliber rifle and loaded the gun. He then crept into his mother's upstairs bedroom. He raised the rifle, taking careful aim as he had done so many times at the shooting range. Then he fired four shots into his mother's head.

Adam Lanza would take 28 lives that day, including 26 people at Sandy Hook Elementary, his mother's, and his own.

Afterward, Lanza prepared to carry out the next part of his plan. Before getting into his mother's car, he dressed in combat gear and what police documents describe as a bulletproof vest. He gathered an assault rifle, a shotgun, two handguns, and enough ammunition to kill hundreds of people. Not forgetting a pair of earplugs, Adam loaded his arsenal into Nancy's black Honda Civic and drove to Sandy Hook Elementary School.

Shooting at the School

Lanza arrived at his childhood school at approximately 9:30 a.m. He drove right up to the front entrance and parked his car in the fire lane. Leaving the shotgun in the car, Lanza carried the other three loaded guns with him as he approached the glass doors to the school. The doors were locked, so Lanza used his semiautomatic

Principal Dawn Hochsprung confronted the shooter in her school.

rifle to shoot through the glass. He quickly entered the school.

Once inside, Lanza wasted little time. In front of him was the principal's office. To his right lay the school cafeteria, where unaware students were rehearsing a play. Lanza strode down the hallway to the left, toward the first-grade classrooms. Before he reached his destination, three women confronted him in the hallway. His noisy entrance had drawn them out of their meeting to investigate. Principal Dawn Hochsprung was the first to encounter Lanza. As she moved toward him in an effort to stop the massacre before it started, Lanza shot her. Close behind Hochsprung was school psychologist Mary Sherlach. She quickly fell to Lanza's gunfire. Of the three women, only lead teacher Natalie Hammond survived.

HOW TO SURVIVE A SCHOOL SHOOTING

School shootings can't always be anticipated or prevented. But students can increase their chances of survival if they know the best ways to stay safe. Most schools practice lockdown drills. Locking down is the best course of action when students and staff are not being directly confronted by a shooter but suspect an escape attempt would put them in the line of fire. In other situations, different actions may offer the best chance for survival. Many experts agree the following strategies are students' best bets in the event of an attack:

- If students see an opportunity to safely escape the building, they should take it. Classroom windows are often good escape routes.

- If escape is not an option, students should hide and lock or barricade themselves in a safe place and turn out the lights. Shooters will likely move on to easier targets. Then immediately call 911 and notify police of the shooter's location so they can neutralize the situation quicker.

- If students come face-to-face with a shooter, their best chance is to try to stop the attacker. Distract the shooter by throwing things or making lots of noise. These strategies work best in large numbers. They can give students a chance to take down the shooter or escape.

Innocence Is Lost

Lanza kept moving, closing in on the first-grade classrooms. The first one he reached belonged to teacher Kaitlin Roig. Knowing her classroom was vulnerable as it was closest to the entrance, Roig had acted immediately to protect her students. Within moments of the first shots, she had turned off the lights in her room and barricaded herself and her first graders inside the classroom's bathroom. As Roig shushed and comforted the children, Lanza walked past.

The next classroom in Lanza's path was substitute teacher Lauren Rousseau's. This time, Lanza entered the room. Rousseau and her aide had not had time to hide their six- and seven-year-old students. Lanza found them huddled together in a corner. Lanza pointed his rifle toward the cluster of children and began shooting. He did not stop until Rousseau, her aide, and all but one of the students were dead. Then Lanza continued down the hall.

He opened the door to Victoria Soto's classroom next. Soto had managed to hide her students—many of them had apparently crowded into a closet. She herself stood to face the gunman. According to reports, when

Lanza demanded to know where her students were, Soto said they were in the auditorium on the other side of the school. But her diversionary tactic did not work. Several of her students made a sudden, desperate attempt to escape. While some of them were able to slip past Lanza unharmed, others fell under rifle fire. Soto and her aide were also killed.

Within five minutes of Lanza entering the school, he had murdered 20 first graders and six staff members. Including his mother, Lanza's victims totaled 27 that day. But he was not quite finished. Lanza was standing in Soto's classroom when the blare of police sirens penetrated his earplugs. Lanza reached for his Glock pistol. Before police could find him, he took his own life. Although he had committed the second-deadliest school shooting in US history, second only to the 2007 shooting at Virginia Tech, Lanza had been far from exhausting his supply of ammunition.[2] Many more would almost certainly have died if local police had not been so quick to react.

Police Respond

The first 911 calls from Sandy Hook Elementary School began pouring in as Adam Lanza began his rampage at

Police and other law enforcement officials began arriving
at the school within minutes of the shooting.

approximately 9:30 a.m. Officers jumped into squad
cars and sped to the scene. They were at the school in
less than three minutes.[3]

The first responders arrived at approximately
9:36 a.m. From the parking lot, they could hear pops of
rifle fire. Some officers saw children running from the
building. The police quickly but carefully entered the
school from various locations. Those who approached
the front entrance noted broken glass as they followed
the sounds of the shooter.

The gunfire soon stopped. Aside from the muffled voices coming over police radios set to low volume, the halls were quiet. Officers were shocked to discover the bodies of Hochsprung and Sherlach near the front of the school. They did not want to believe such violence was possible in their peaceful suburban town. They pushed past the first victims and began a methodical search of the rest of the school. The officers took locked doors as a sign those inside were safe, and they called for ambulances in anticipation of wounded victims.

A Devastating Scene

As the Newtown police officers moved through the front of the school, they soon came upon Soto's first-grade classroom.

Nothing could prepare them for what they were about to see. "One look, and your life was absolutely changed," recalled Officer Michael McGowan.[4] Lanza lay dead inside the door with his guns beside him. Beyond Lanza lay the lifeless bodies of several children and two adults.

The police, unsure whether Lanza was the only gunman, watched for signs of danger as they began checking over the bodies one by one. They held out hope that some of the victims might still be clinging to life. One little girl was— but barely. Her faint pulse and shallow breathing told Officer William Chapman she might not have much time. He immediately scooped her up and rushed her out to one of the ambulances that had begun to arrive at the scene. As he ran, he

A SAFE HAVEN

Some students fled the school. Six of them appeared outside 69-year-old Gene Rosen's house, stopping quietly in a circle near the end of his driveway. A bus driver was with them, agitatedly repeating that everything was all right. When Rosen approached the children, he saw they were frightened and crying. The bus driver told him something had happened at the school. Rosen brought them inside and listened to their story. They told him their teacher, Ms. Soto, was dead, and that there had been a man with a big gun and a small gun. Rosen brought the children juice and offered them some of the toys he kept for his grandson. Having calmed the children a little, he contacted their parents to let them know their children were safe and waiting to be picked up.

told her, "You're safe now; your parents love you."[5] But the little girl was not safe. She would be among the lost.

Inside the school, officers moved on to the classroom adjacent to Soto's. They were devastated to find approximately twice as many limp bodies there, the vast majority of them six- and seven-year-old children. Miraculously, one uninjured child emerged. After confirming the gunman was dead, Officer Leonard Penna led the traumatized girl out of the building to a triage area.

No One to Save

As the police were conducting their search of Sandy Hook, ambulances and emergency medical teams gathered in the school parking lot. They waited, ready to begin treating the victims of the shooting. A couple of wounded victims were led to the triage area. Medical personnel applied first aid before rushing them to a local hospital. The rest of the medical team watched

"I stood outside waiting to go [into the school], but a police officer came out and said they didn't need any nurses, so I knew it wasn't good."[6]
—Hospital nurse Maureen Kerins, who hoped to offer her skills in the wake of the tragedy at Sandy Hook

and waited for other injured survivors to come out of the school. None came.

Eventually, a call came in with word that no more ambulances or medical expertise would be needed. There was no one else to save. And yet, there were other ways to help. On the opposite side of the yellow tape blocking off the crime scene were the parents who did not know if they would ever see their children again. Many of the medical personnel stayed with the parents, offering what comfort and reassurance they could.

Evacuation

With the gunman confirmed dead and any wounded being cared for, the police began evacuating the school.

MASS SHOOTINGS

One of the first school shootings to truly rock the nation through televised broadcasts occurred on April 20, 1999, at Columbine High School in Littleton, Colorado. Students Eric Harris and Dylan Klebold killed 13 and wounded 21 others before committing suicide.[7] On April 16, 2007, a massacre at Virginia Tech became the deadliest school shooting in US history. Student Seung-Hui Cho killed 32 and wounded 17 more.[8] Then he took his own life. Another shooting occurred at a movie theater in Aurora, Colorado, on July 20, 2012. James Holmes, 24, fatally shot 12 and wounded 58 others during a showing of The Dark Knight Rises.[9]

All these events drew heavy media coverage, leading to fears the attention might inspire other killers. They also prompted nationwide discussions about how to improve security in public buildings, especially schools.

At each locked classroom door, they yelled "Police! Police!" and told those inside it was safe to come out.[10] Many teachers thought this might be a ploy by violent gunmen. They refused to open their doors until the police proved their identities. Ripping off their badges, the officers slid them under doors and pressed them to windows. A current of relief flowed through the school as authorities began leading children out of the building.

Officers and teachers spoke in soothing voices as they coaxed the children into organized lines. They told them everything would be okay. Then they asked the students to close their eyes. The frightened children squeezed their eyes shut, tightly grasped the shoulder or hand of the person in front of them, and trusted the adults to lead them to safety. As the children shuffled past, several officers positioned themselves in front of the bodies in the hallway and first-grade classrooms to block the awful scenes. Once the survivors of Sandy Hook were safely outside, authorities led them down the road to the firehouse.

Children were led out of the school holding onto each other in lines.

CHAPTER
FOUR

THE TRUTH SINKS IN

Starting around 10:00 a.m., parents whose children attended Sandy Hook had begun receiving automated phone calls about a possible emergency in Newtown. At first, they knew only that all the schools were in lockdown and there had been reports of a shooter in the town. Soon the message came that the shooter had been inside one of the schools. And finally, they learned the name of the school: Sandy Hook Elementary.

As cell phones rang and televisions and radios spewed vague but ominous details, hundreds of cars jammed Newtown's streets. Parents abandoned their vehicles and sprinted toward the school. Authorities directed them to the firehouse.

Worried friends and family members gathered near the school waiting for news.

Reunion

Inside the firehouse was barely restrained chaos—a whirlwind of children, teachers, parents, police, and others. Teachers were focused on calming their terrified students. They had their classes sit on the floor, organized by grade, so the authorities could count heads and parents could easily find their children. Most of the children had at least a general understanding of what had happened—some were sobbing, others were quiet. "When we were going out of the school, we kinda knew that a lot of people were hurt and killed. It was scary," recalled first grader Shayne Frate.[1]

Some parents found their children right away, relief cutting through the grim atmosphere. Many immediately contacted the parents of other children they recognized. Other parents ran from room to room, not finding their children, demanding to know if anyone had seen them or their teachers. A few got word their children had escaped the building and had been taken in elsewhere. For the other 20 families—and for the relatives of the six staff members who were missing—it was the beginning of the longest day of their lives.

Reality

As the clock ticked on toward noon, families still missing their loved ones watched parents and children slowly filter out of the firehouse. Eventually, they were ushered into a separate room. Police officers asked them to provide names and descriptions of their relatives. Then they settled in to wait for news.

> "It's very hard to console parents in this situation. There's no theological answer to this. What you have to do is hug them and just be with them and cry with them."[2]
> —Grief counselor Rabbi Shaul Praver

Grief counselors and clergy members did their best to help ease parents' anxiety. Connecticut governor Dannel Malloy was also there to offer his support. Well-meaning members of the community set out food, but it was left untouched. Some families prayed as they waited. Others simply clung to the hope their loved one was still out there somewhere, injured or hiding, but alive.

Eventually, law enforcement announced the staggering death toll of the shooting. The quiet room convulsed in grief, with people sobbing, shrieking, and collapsing into one another's arms. But no answers were given, and no names were yet spoken. Family members were asked to provide photographs of their missing loved ones to help identify the victims. As the afternoon stretched on, each parent still hoped his or her child had survived.

The Community Gathers

News of the deaths of so many neighbors and friends spread quickly through the tight-knit Newtown community. People filed into places of worship for comfort and to pray for the victims and their families. Business owners replaced signs advertising daily specials with messages of support and hope.

Together, the people of Newtown tried to process the horror and senselessness of what had happened. They speculated about who could have taken so many innocent lives. They wondered which faces they would never see again, and they dreaded hearing their names. The dead would not be strangers to any in the

"Sandy Hook is such a tight-knit community, everybody knew everybody's face. Right when the parents came in and they had the frantic look on their face[s], everybody said, 'I see your daughter, she's okay' or 'Your son is here, don't worry.'"[3]

—Valerie Frate, mother of a student at Sandy Hook Elementary School small town. "We'll know all of them," said business owner Bonnie Fredericks.[4]

First Responders Recover

While families waited in the firehouse, Newtown's first responders were struggling to recover from what they had seen that day. Scenes from the day flashed through their minds. For some, it would be the beginning of a long battle with post-traumatic stress disorder (PTSD).

SANDY HOOK AND POST-TRAUMATIC STRESS DISORDER

Post-traumatic stress disorder (PTSD) is a condition of extreme stress or anxiety triggered by witnessing or experiencing a traumatic event. Symptoms can include having nightmares or flashbacks about the event, avoiding reminders of the event, and having trouble focusing on daily tasks. People with PTSD also tend to startle easily and have difficulty sleeping. Some adults and children are quick to anger and have outbursts or other behavioral problems.

Several of those who were present for the shooting or its aftermath at Sandy Hook are now suffering from PTSD. Those who witnessed the carnage firsthand are particularly vulnerable. For many Newtown police officers, it has been impossible to return to normal. Some have been unable to work since the tragedy due to PTSD; others returned to work only to leave again. There is no good long-term solution for Newtown's traumatized workers. PTSD treatment and workers' compensation is expensive. Relief funds covered officers' expenses in the months after the tragedy, and Governor Malloy helped to set up a fund for continued support. Nonetheless, workers may face a struggle to get the ongoing mental health care they need.

In addition to the horror was guilt. Both law enforcement and medical professionals replayed their actions that day over and over again. They wondered whether maybe, if they had only arrived sooner or moved faster, more victims would still be alive. Police Chief Michael Kehoe was torn by conflicted feelings about the day. He said,

> You feel a sense of guilt that you weren't there quick enough to [save them], but I also know that our response stopped that threat . . . and [the shooter] could not proceed any further.[5]

Closure

Hours after learning many of their loved ones lay dead inside Sandy Hook Elementary School, families were still waiting for confirmation that their child, sibling, or spouse was among them. They knew some victims had been treated at the hospital, and this fact kept their hope alive. However, parents sensed officials were keeping the truth from them, and they could not stand not knowing any longer.

Governor Malloy was aware that of the 26 victims of the shooting, only two had been taken to the hospital, and the likelihood they had survived was slim. He knew

Connecticut governor Dannel Malloy continued his support for the victims' families, speaking at a memorial service later that night.

every minute that passed was extending their families' painful false hope. Around 3:00 p.m., Malloy spoke to Colonel Danny Stebbins, the commander of the state police. He confirmed none of the children being treated at the hospital had survived. And although the bodies had not been positively identified, Malloy felt it was wrong to delay giving these families the closure they sought.

So when parents began pleading for honest information, Malloy took it upon himself to give it to them. He stood in that solemn firehouse room, looking at the parents' desperate faces. And he told them their loved ones would not be coming back.

Screams tore through the air, and people fell to the floor. As the inconsolable families regained their footing, some of them numbly headed home. Others stayed late into the night, unwilling to let go of hope until it was confirmed beyond a doubt their missing family member was gone. By the early hours of the morning, all the deceased had been identified. There was no room left for hope—only for grief.

The Nation Stands with Newtown

News of the tragedy in Newtown struck a chord in hearts across the nation. Millions watched in shock and horror as the chaotic scenes at the school crowded their television screens. Parents everywhere felt the deepest pain for those who had lost their children. President Barack Obama was one of those sympathetic parents.

At 3:15 p.m., a somber president addressed the nation, offering condolences and expressing a need for positive change. He wiped tears from his eyes as he spoke about the victims. Then he gave voice to the nation's grief:

Our hearts are broken today—for the parents and grandparents, sisters and brothers of these little children, and for the families of the adults who were lost. Our hearts are broken for the parents of the survivors as well, for as blessed as they are to have their children home tonight, they know that their children's innocence has been torn away from them too early, and there are no words that will ease their pain.[6]

Obama highlighted the importance of uniting as Americans, both in showing compassion for Newtown families and in an effort to prevent similar tragedies from happening in the future. He closed by asking God to "heal the brokenhearted and bind up their wounds."[7]

SOCIAL MEDIA MISINFORMATION

Popular social media Web sites Twitter and Facebook were among the first forums for people to share reactions and information about the shooting. Social media feeds were overwhelmed with sympathy for the families of Sandy Hook, outrage at the tragedy, and calls for better gun control and security measures.

People also used these sites to share news, but some of the initial media reports proved incorrect.

Early reports said the shooter was related to one of the teachers at the school. They also speculated the shooter was Ryan Lanza, Adam Lanza's older brother. This piece of misinformation was magnified when Facebook users shared the elder Lanza's photo almost 10,000 times within five hours and attacked him in comments.[8] Ryan defended himself on Facebook, updating his status to say, "It wasn't me."[9]

Mourners gathered for a candlelit vigil on the night of the shooting.

Newtown Unites

Shortly after the president's statement, with the winter sun hanging low in the background, Governor Malloy and state police spokesman Lieutenant J. Paul Vance briefed the media with what little information could be released at the time. Vance confirmed a death toll of 27 at the school including the shooter, plus the additional death of someone at the shooter's home.

As dusk fell, investigators went to work inside the school. Some grieving families still remained at the firehouse. Outside, crowds gathered for media briefings held at approximately 5:00 and 6:00 p.m., but little new information was released. Malloy offered words of reassurance, saying, "It's too early to speak of recovery, but . . . we're all in this together. We'll do whatever we can to overcome this event. We will get through it."[10]

Hundreds gathered for a vigil at Saint Rose of Lima Roman Catholic Church near Sandy Hook Elementary School, where the altar held a candle for each of the 26 victims from the school. Crowds of mourners filled the church and surrounded the building, many holding candles. They cried, embraced, and held hands. They sang and prayed together. And they listened to the consoling words of parish priest Monsignor Robert Weiss and Governor Malloy as the men tried to begin healing a broken community.

CHAPTER
FIVE

GRIEF AND REMEMBRANCE

The people of Newtown awoke to a different world the morning of December 15, 2012. Over the next days, weeks, and months, the community would receive an outpouring of love and sympathy from around the world. They would find ways to remember their lost ones, and they would lay their children and teachers to rest. By Saturday morning, all those who had lost their lives in the shooting had been identified. Their names, painfully familiar to the small community of Newtown, were released to the public later that day.

Makeshift Memorials

Memorials appeared throughout the town in the days following the shooting. Lit candles surrounded growing piles of angel ornaments, flowers, stuffed animals, cards, and balloons outside Sandy Hook Elementary School, the firehouse, and other landmarks throughout

Mourners built memorials outside the school and around town.

the town. A large memorial overtook the center of the town, where many from neighboring communities came to pay their respects.

Art teacher Eric Mueller transformed a hillside into a host of wooden angels painted to represent the victims. Others affixed the victims' names to fence posts, flags, banners, and religious symbols. All over town, people hung signs in shop windows and propped them in yards. So many heartfelt gifts, donations, and condolences flooded in from around the world that Newtown officials were forced to ask people to stop sending them.

THE VICTIMS

Charlotte Bacon, 6

Daniel Barden, 7

Rachel D'Avino, 29

Olivia Engel, 6

Josephine Gay, 7

Dawn Hochsprung, 47

Dylan Hockley, 6

Madeleine Hsu, 6

Catherine Hubbard, 6

Chase Kowalski, 7

Jesse Lewis, 6

Ana Marquez-Greene, 6

James Mattioli, 6

Grace McDonnell, 7

Anne Marie Murphy, 52

Emilie Parker, 6

Jack Pinto, 6

Noah Pozner, 6

Caroline Previdi, 6

Jessica Rekos, 6

Avielle Richman, 6

Lauren Rousseau, 30

Mary Sherlach, 56

Victoria Soto, 27

Benjamin Wheeler, 6

Allison Wyatt, 6

President Obama spoke with the family of teacher Victoria Soto at the interfaith memorial service.

A Faithful Community

Members of the community looked forward to reuniting with their friends and neighbors at the interfaith memorial service to be held at Newtown High School on the evening of Sunday, December 16. Adding to the anticipation, President Obama was scheduled to speak.

When the president arrived at Newtown High School, his first priority was to meet with the families who had been most deeply affected by the tragedy. Obama hugged grieving parents and held excited children. He also left a note on a classroom whiteboard that read, "You're in our thoughts and prayers."[1]

Meanwhile, hundreds of people streamed into the high school auditorium. Applause broke out as Sandy Hook's first responders entered the room, and children were handed stuffed animals as they walked to their seats. By the time the service began late that evening, the auditorium held 900 people. Another 1,300 spilled into a nearby room.[2]

The opening words floated out over the hushed auditorium just before 8:00 p.m. "We needed this. We needed to be together," said Reverend Matthew Crebbin, minister of the Newtown Congregational Church.[3] His greeting was followed by prayers and readings of scripture from a number of faiths, including Judaism, Christianity, Islam, and Baha'i. Jason Graves of Newtown's Al Hedaya Islamic Center summed up the purpose of the service with his prayer: "We ask God to grant those lost a special place in paradise. And we ask that their families be given the strength to endure the unendurable."[4]

When President Obama took the stage, he came with "the love and prayers of a nation," letting the people of Newtown know they were not alone in their grief. "All across this land of ours, we have wept with you," said the president.[5] He talked about Newtown's inspiring atmosphere of love in the face of extreme violence. And he admitted the United States was not doing enough to prevent similar tragedies. After a call to action, Obama closed by speaking the names of the 20 lost children. "God has called them all home," he said. "For those of us who remain, let us find the strength to carry on, and make our country worthy of their memory."[6]

> "This is our first task, caring for our children. . . . That's how, as a society, we will be judged. And by that measure . . . can we honestly say that we're doing enough to keep our children, all of them, safe from harm? . . . If we're honest with ourselves, the answer's no. We're not doing enough. And we will have to change."[7]
> —President Barack Obama at the interfaith memorial service in Newtown

At Rest

The next day, many Newtown residents wore clothing or ribbons of green and white—Sandy Hook Elementary School's colors—as a sign of remembrance and unity. Others dressed in somber black. Friends and neighbors joined the families of Noah Pozner and Jack Pinto as they laid the first of the victims to rest.

Noah's mother spoke with passion and strength at Noah's funeral service. Speaking directly to Noah, she fondly remembered her son's love of tacos and his

People around the country built memorials to the victims, including this one in Pearland, Texas.

mischievous nature. "I can only believe that you were planted on Earth to bloom in heaven," she said.[8] Jack was buried in his favorite football player's jersey.

A seemingly endless string of funerals kept Newtown in an attitude of mourning for the entire week leading up to Christmas. Victoria Soto's funeral Wednesday was the first for an adult who had been lost. Hundreds attended the service at Lordship Community Church, half of them standing outside in the cold. Bagpipe music played as numerous state police officers escorted Soto's coffin into the church. The beloved teacher was universally praised for her selflessness, heroism, and goofy sense of humor. Musician Paul Simon performed Simon and Garfunkel's melancholy song "The Sound of Silence" as part of the service.

Grace McDonnell's funeral was one of several on Thursday. Her family doodled images of everything she loved all over her white coffin. Jesse Lewis, also buried Thursday, was remembered for his bravery in trying to help his classmates reach safety.

Friday morning at 9:30 a.m., exactly a week after the first shots rang out at Sandy Hook, Newtown observed a moment of silence. It was broken only by the sound of the rain and the tolling of a bell from a nearby church rung 26 times.

REMEMBERING NANCY LANZA

In the aftermath of the Sandy Hook shooting, Nancy Lanza's death was all but forgotten. Memorials with 26 names sprouted up all over Newtown. Bells tolled 26 times for the victims of Newtown the week after the shooting. But Lanza had killed 27 that day. The first victim was his mother.

Why did so few include Nancy Lanza in their remembrances of the lost? Many laid partial blame on her for raising Adam. They blamed her for introducing him to guns and for not getting him the psychological help they assumed he must have needed. Nonetheless, family and close friends held a memorial for Nancy on December 20. Months later, a funeral service was held in New Hampshire. Nancy's sister said the funeral was delayed out of respect for the other victims and their families.

Numerous funerals were held later that day, including a service for Dylan Hockley, the child whom special education teacher Anne Marie Murphy had died trying to protect. Mourners wore purple, Dylan's favorite color, and they released a purple balloon for each child lost in the tragedy.

Saturday, December 22, brought the final funeral services for Sandy Hook's children. Approximately 1,000 people attended Ana Marquez-Greene's music-filled funeral, which included a performance by jazz artist Harry Connick Jr.[9] Children Josephine Gay and Emilie Parker were also laid to rest on Saturday.

Christmas

While the community mourned the lost, residents did some last-minute Christmas shopping the weekend before the holiday. It was really for the children that Newtown felt at all able to celebrate the winter holidays. And so Newtown families bought and wrapped gifts and set them under trees. Strangers embraced in the streets, and cards and paper snowflakes sent from around the country drifted into Sandy Hook's post office box. Waking up on Christmas morning, parents held their

Newtown residents celebrated the holiday season with grief.

children close and told them they loved them before allowing them to open their gifts.

Three days after Christmas, town roads were closed while the families of Sandy Hook victims visited memorials to their loved ones. Town official Patricia Llodra had announced it would be their last chance to do so before the memorials were cleared away. The materials were to be recycled and used in building a permanent memorial. On December 28, family members collected the mementos that meant the most to them. Then, in the night, the cherished memorials disappeared. The community of Newtown was beginning to move on.

CHAPTER
SIX

SEEKING ANSWERS

With the somber task of burying their dead behind them, Newtown joined people around the world in questioning why the tragedy had happened. Lanza's rampage was different from other widely publicized school shootings in which gunmen had targeted their own schools and their own classmates. Why would a young man enter an elementary school and gun down dozens of strangers, the majority of them innocent children? Why would he also kill his mother, the only person with whom he had a connection? It simply did not make sense.

But the grieving people of Newtown needed to understand. They needed to make a plan so they could better protect their children from violence. And so they, along with others across the globe, began searching for answers where none could be easily found.

The world wanted to know what motivated Lanza's attack.

Access to Guns

One issue that immediately jumped to the forefront of the discussion about the Newtown shooting was gun control legislation. In addition to the guns Lanza brought to Sandy Hook Elementary School, investigators found a large arsenal of firearms and other weapons in his home. Lanza clearly had easy access to weapons that were capable of killing large numbers of people.

After the school shootings in Columbine, Colorado, in 1999 and at Virginia Tech in 2007, many gun control advocates focused on the failings and loopholes in the National Instant Criminal Background Check System (NICS). The NICS is meant to prevent criminals and other potentially dangerous people from owning weapons. In Lanza's case, however, all the guns found with him at the school and in his home had been legally obtained by his mother. Was Nancy's choice to expose her son to and involve him in her shooting hobby a mistake?

WAS LANZA ON DRUGS?

While Lanza may have been prescribed medications or used recreational drugs at some point, investigators found no traces of drugs in his system after the shooting. The toxicology tests screened for alcohol, marijuana, and other illegal drugs, in addition to antidepressants, antipsychotics, and other prescription medications.

People for and against increased gun control rallied outside the National Shooting Sports Foundation headquarters, which is located in Newtown.

Perhaps. Regardless, even strict gun control laws— short of banning guns altogether—likely would not have stopped Lanza's rampage.

Mental Illness

Others questioned whether Lanza's apparent mental challenges drove him to this act of violence. Although the diagnoses of sensory processing disorder and Asperger's syndrome a family member reported have not been confirmed, Lanza's extreme social awkwardness and unusual reactions to noise and physical touch caused many to believe Lanza was indeed mentally ill. The media seized on these speculations, implying Lanza's

DARK DRAWINGS?

One of Nancy Lanza's friends reportedly claimed Nancy had been disturbed by drawings she found in her son's room. "One [drawing] had a woman clutching a religious item, like rosary beads, and holding a child, and she was getting all shot up in the back with blood flying everywhere," recalled the friend.[1] He claimed Nancy had not yet confronted her son and was unsure what to do about the drawings. The friend's story has not been proven one way or the other.

Police did find drawings among Adam's personal belongings. However, the content of those drawings had not been revealed to the public as of August 2013.

mental condition may have predisposed him to violent behavior. In reality, there is no evidence supporting a connection between violent behavior and Asperger's syndrome or similar disorders.

If Lanza struggled with other psychological issues that might have triggered his rampage, history likely will never know it. In the cases of the Columbine and Virginia Tech shooters, their personal writings revealed their mental states in the time leading up to their violent actions. Investigators are hopeful a collection of Lanza's journals and drawings may provide insight into his mental state. Details from the investigation are not expected to be released until the fall of 2013.

Journals shed some light on the thought processes of Columbine shooters Eric Harris, *left*, and Dylan Klebold.

A Social Outcast

It is a long-held stereotype that potential killers are often loners. But millions of people have social difficulties without becoming mass murderers. It is hard to know how Lanza felt about his social isolation. If he felt constant, deep-cutting rejection, then that might have contributed to whatever anguish caused him to strike out. But he might have simply felt more comfortable when he was alone.

A family member reportedly claimed the boy had often come home bruised from Sandy Hook Elementary

MILITARY DREAMS

Nancy Lanza's friend Marvin LaFontaine recalled that Adam wanted to be a Marine from a young age. He looked up to his uncle James Champion, a military veteran. Champion was trained as a member of the US Army Special Forces, known informally as the Green Berets. A childhood photo shows Adam dressed for Halloween in a military costume. LaFontaine said when it became clear a military career would not be possible for Lanza due to his social difficulties, Nancy began discouraging the idea.

School—that he had apparently been bullied or otherwise abused there. However, this account is unsubstantiated and likely sensationalized. Others close to Lanza have said he did not appear to be bullied, but rather that people tended to leave him alone. Regardless, the vast majority of those who are bullied do not choose to kill innocent people. Bullying by itself could not have caused Lanza's actions.

Another unfounded theory that attracted media attention claimed Lanza felt rejected by his mother. According to an individual with no clear connection to Lanza, Nancy had been planning to institutionalize him, and Lanza found out about her plans. If this were true, feelings of rejection could generate rage—possibly even homicidal rage. However, more reliable sources state Nancy was planning a cross-country move so Lanza could attend a college suited to his needs. When asked why, Nancy reportedly replied, "You never turn your back on your children."[2] Whatever Lanza's feelings might have been about the move, there is no proof his mother ever rejected him.

A Culture of Violence: Video Games

In addition to Lanza's exposure to guns and shooting, he seems to have enjoyed playing violent video games. Investigators found a large amount of gaming equipment in his home, and several sources have reported he spent a lot of time playing games such as *Call of Duty*, a war-themed first-person shooter game.

There is no way to know for certain what role if any these video games played in Lanza's life. Violent video games have long been popular among

PREDISPOSITION TO VIOLENCE?

Researchers at the University of Connecticut accepted a request to study Lanza's genes. It is believed they are trying to understand whether genetics might predispose some people to committing acts of violence. Experts think geneticists at the university will be looking for mutations or other unusual features of Lanza's genes that might help them answer that question.

The study is controversial. Some experts worry the research risks finding a false connection between violence and certain genetic mutations. People with those mutations could end up being feared for no reason. Others feel genetic research into violence has been a long time coming. This is the first time geneticists have studied the DNA of a mass murderer in detail.

Although some would argue violent video games should be regulated or banned instead of guns, video games alone cannot be blamed for the Newtown school shooting.

young people, yet hardly anyone acts out these fantasies. However, it is possible violent media including games have a stronger influence on a very small number of people. According to psychologist Peter Langman, "Kids who commit rampage attacks often do have a fascination or preoccupation with violent media. They do not just play violent video games; they become obsessed with them."[3] We don't know whether Lanza approached this level of preoccupation with video games. But video games alone cannot be blamed for Lanza's actions.

A Culture of Violence: Glory Killing

Music, books, art, movies, and television are also guilty of glorifying violence and risk influencing potential mass shooters. Perpetrators of violence are often portrayed as powerful, respected, and hypermasculine, all traits many school shooters feel they are lacking. When young people—especially young men—struggle with extreme insecurities, it is not surprising some of them turn to violence to compensate.

It is unclear whether Lanza felt violence was necessary to protect his identity or cover insecurities. In any case, it might seem the idea of turning mass murder into a public spectacle appealed to him. Media attention can reinforce the message that extreme acts of violence can be a path to a kind of fame. Due to the fact that Lanza had saved at least one article about another mass murder, some speculate he might have been inspired, at least in part, by others who committed similar rampage attacks. Despite speculation in the media following the shooting, there is no clear proof whether Lanza was motivated by any of these factors.

Waiting for Answers

Until Connecticut police piece together more evidence, speculating is all even experts can do. We are left with many questions: Was Lanza a victim of misguided parenting? Was he influenced by an overexposure to

COPYCATS

One of the primary fears about heavy media coverage of mass murders is that it will spark "copycat" events. Other potential killers sometimes see violent events in the media and hold up the perpetrators as their role models. They become determined to commit a similar crime.

One case of this was seen in the shootings at Virginia Tech. In the manifesto shooter Seung-Hui Cho provided to the media, he wrote, "Generation after generation, we martyrs, like [Columbine shooters] Eric and Dylan, will sacrifice our lives to [get revenge] for what you Apostles of Sin have done to us."[4] This suggests the Columbine massacre inspired the deadliest mass shooting in the United States. Columbine and other mass murders might have likewise inspired Lanza to act.

guns and violent media? Or could he have been taking revenge on the world for childhood bullying? Was Lanza dangerously insecure, desperate for attention and a sense of power? Perhaps society failed a youth whose mental or emotional health was in far more fragile a state than anyone could have foreseen.

We still do not have the answers. It is very possible Lanza was driven by something no one has yet been able to guess. But it is equally possible we will never know the true motivation behind Lanza's rampage.

Action Allianc

ONGRES

's Your Turr

CHAPTER
SEVEN

TAKING ACTION

In the wake of the shooting at Sandy Hook, there was a public outcry for action. People wanted assurance no tragedy of this magnitude would ever be allowed to happen again. They turned to their legislators, calling for changes in gun control, mental health, and school safety policies. Most of the national conversation centered on gun legislation. It was a polarizing issue, and numerous politicians spoke out on both sides of the debate.

Those in favor of stricter gun laws argued military-style assault weapons do not belong in the hands of ordinary citizens and high-capacity magazines are not necessary for responsible recreational gun use. They also felt background checks were not rigorous enough and hoped to close loopholes allowing people to buy guns unchecked at gun shows or to purchase guns for others who were unable to do so legally. As criminal justice experts Jaclyn Schildkraut and Tiffany Cox Hernandez noted:

Newtown residents called for change at a national level.

There are still over a million cases of diagnosed mental illness and institutionalization that have yet to be reported to the [NICS]. Therefore, it is virtually impossible to know if any of the people passing background checks each year should not be eligible to do so because of mental illness. Further, due to the lack of restrictions on private sellers, including at gun shows, there is no way to trace how many of these transactions include sales to people who do not actually meet the criteria for legal gun ownership.[1]

SCHOOL SAFETY

School safety remained an important but comparatively low-profile concern after Sandy Hook. The parents of first-grade victims Emilie Parker and Josephine Gay recognized flaws in the security system at Sandy Hook Elementary School. With other parents, they started the organization Safe and Sound to encourage other communities to take action regarding their schools' safety.

Legislation that was passed in Connecticut after the tragedy included the creation of the Sandy Hook Advisory Commission, a panel that would help strengthen weaknesses in school security. One of the commission's recommendations was to ensure all classroom doors could be locked from the inside.

Other cities and states also made school safety changes in the months after December 14. Many hired more school security staff. Some considered protecting their schools with armed guards or training teachers to use firearms. Many also discussed making structural changes to schools, such as installing better cameras or adding more physical barriers to threats. However, making these changes would be costly.

President Obama promised to make gun control a priority. He emphasized the need for common sense and responsible gun ownership.

Equally determined were those who wanted to protect US citizens' right to bear arms. They argued none of the measures suggested by gun control advocates would have made a difference in the case of Sandy Hook, nor would they be likely to make a difference in preventing similar tragedies. Many felt the real problem was that the nation was not doing enough to identify and help people with mental health challenges. Republican leaders tended to agree stricter gun laws would be counterproductive.

Promises and Polarization

About a month after the shooting, family members of 11 of the victims helped organize a group called Sandy Hook Promise. The goal of the group was to make the country a safer place through changes informed by love, compassion, common sense, and listening to opposing viewpoints. They wanted Newtown "to be remembered not as the town filled with grief and victims; but as the place where real change began."[2] Although these families wanted to focus on healing, they recognized they had

The parents of victim Benjamin Wheeler became members of Sandy Hook Promise.

a short window of opportunity to push for change. The public emotions of sorrow, fury, and fear were raw, and people were ready to take action to protect their own children and communities.

The group did not immediately take a stand on the issues being heatedly debated by politicians. They allowed themselves time to learn more about gun control, mental health, school safety, and other issues so when it came time to act, they would be well informed. While remaining politically neutral, Sandy Hook Promise members supported the president in starting the national conversation they hoped would lead to addressing these issues.

Yet as time went on and gun control continued to be the focus of discussions about violence prevention, more Newtown families—including members of Sandy Hook Promise—began voicing strong opinions. Many spoke at a series of public gun control hearings in Connecticut at the end of January. The majority of the victims' family members who were present came out in favor of stricter gun laws. Benjamin Wheeler's father, David, argued:

> Thomas Jefferson described our inalienable rights as life, liberty, and the pursuit of happiness. I do not think the order of those important words was haphazard and casual. The liberty of any person to own a military assault weapon and high-capacity magazine and to keep them in their home is second to the right of my son to his life.[3]

FRANCINE WHEELER ADDRESSES THE NATION

On April 13, 2013, Francine Wheeler, mother of Benjamin, became the first person besides President Obama and Vice President Biden to deliver the White House's weekly address during the Obama administration. Appearing with her husband, Wheeler shared their still-fresh grief about the death of their son. With tears in her eyes, she said,

> In the four months since we lost our loved ones, thousands of other Americans have died at the end of a gun. Thousands of other families across the United States are also drowning in our grief.[4]

Wheeler pleaded with US citizens to talk to their senators and take action in supporting gun control reforms. Before signing off, she asked viewers to "help this be the moment when real change begins."[5]

Others, including Mark Mattioli, James's father, disagreed. Mattioli countered, "I think there's much more promise . . . for identifying, researching, and creating solutions along the lines of mental health."[6] Despite everyone's best intentions, it would prove difficult even for those closest to the tragedy to find enough common ground to initiate large-scale changes.

Change Sweeps the States

In his State of the Union address on February 12, 2013, President Obama asked both gun control and Second Amendment supporters to come together in support of what he called commonsense gun laws. As violence continued claiming more lives through the winter and spring, the gun control debate continued in states across the country. Some states moved toward more limitations on gun and ammunition sales, while others pushed to allow more of their residents to carry guns. With the Sandy Hook shooting still fresh in their minds, Connecticut lawmakers worked throughout the rest of February and March on a gun bill they felt would keep their citizens safe.

On April 4, Governor Malloy signed that bill into law. It included an extensive assault weapons ban, a limit on how many bullets were allowed in an ammunition clip, and more rigorous background checks, among other measures. Other states, including Colorado, New York, and Maryland, also tightened gun laws in response to Newtown's tragedy. At the same time, approximately three times as many states expanded gun freedoms, including North and South Dakota, Arkansas, Kentucky, and Oklahoma.

Stalemate in Washington

On April 8, Newtown victim family members joined President Obama as he delivered a passionate plea for national gun control legislation. Nicole Hockley, mother of Dylan, introduced the president. "Do something before our tragedy becomes your tragedy," she urged.[7] During his speech, Obama pressed for action, noting that measures such as

CONNECTICUT GUN LAW REVISIONS

Approximately two months after Connecticut passed stricter gun laws, legislators approved a series of revisions to those laws. The revisions included a proposal to allow people to retain assault weapons they had purchased on or before April 4, 2013. They also aimed to allow more law enforcement officers to carry assault weapons. Overall, the revisions were meant to clarify and elaborate on aspects of the legislation that were confusing or vague. Governor Malloy had not yet signed the bill for the proposed changes as of August 2013.

Nelba Marquez-Greene, *right*, with her husband Jimmy Greene, called for reform in the way people with mental illness are treated.

expanding background checks drew the support of up to 90 percent of US citizens.[8]

Obama and many Sandy Hook families supported amendments including bans on assault weapons, limits on magazine capacities, and universal background checks. Over the following weeks, the US Senate failed to pass any of them.

Obama addressed the public again on April 17, surrounded by Sandy Hook parents. Obama chastised Congress and lobbyist group the National Rifle Association for blocking these "commonsense" measures.[9] He vowed to keep fighting to enact changes that would save American lives, and he urged supporters to speak up.

Months later, neither gun control advocates nor Second Amendment supporters showed signs of backing down or reaching a compromise. On the six-month anniversary of the tragedy in Newtown, victims' families again journeyed to Washington, DC, to lobby for gun control. They could not tell whether the changes they sought were on the horizon.

Mental Health

In the months after December 14, mental health and school safety took a backseat to gun control in the national conversation about violence prevention. Many advocates of mental health reform, including some Sandy Hook parents, worked to raise awareness about the issue.

In an interview on the television program *60 Minutes* that aired on April 7, some victims' families agreed improving mental health care was just as important as implementing new gun laws. Nelba Marquez-Greene, a marriage and family therapist, voiced her concern about the stigma surrounding mental illness in the United

States. She said it was one of the main things preventing people from getting the help they need.

That spring, Marquez-Greene helped promote a proposal for new legislation that would improve mental health care for children. Mark Mattioli also continued asserting that mental health was a more practical focus for violence prevention efforts than gun control. The parents of another Newtown victim, first grader Avielle Richman, drew on their medical backgrounds to garner support for research on the brain health of violent individuals.

"I Am Adam Lanza's Mother"

Sandy Hook parents were not the only ones seeking better mental health care solutions. Parents of violent or suicidal children across the country were perhaps even more desperate for help. They did not want their child to become the next Adam Lanza.

Shortly after the shooting, blogger Liza Long posted an essay about her 13-year-old son whose violent rages were out of control. He had even pulled a knife on her after she suggested he return some overdue library books. Although most children with mental health challenges do not become violent, Long felt her son's episodes of extreme violence were the result of mental illness. After relating a recent terrifying episode, Long wrote:

> I am sharing this story because I am Adam Lanza's mother. I am Dylan Klebold's and Eric Harris's mother. . . . I am Seung-Hui Cho's mother. And these boys—and their mothers—need help. In the wake of another horrific national tragedy, it's easy to talk about guns. But it's time to talk about mental illness.[10]

Long's bravery in going public with her controversial struggles spurred other families to join the conversation about mental health.

By the six-month anniversary of the shooting, although discussions about violence prevention were still heated, no changes had been made at the national level. Victims' families and politicians continued lobbying for the issues important to them. Would the tragedy in Newtown inspire nationwide changes? Only time will tell.

MENTAL HEALTH AWARENESS

On June 3, President Obama brought further awareness to the issue of mental health by hosting a conference at the White House. He emphasized how common mental illness was, yet how few people sought treatment. Obama asked for help in "bringing mental illness out of the shadows," in erasing the shame and encouraging people to seek treatment for mental illnesses just as they would for other diseases or injuries.[11]

CHAPTER
EIGHT

MOVING FORWARD

Before Sandy Hook parents immersed themselves in politics and policy, they had to take a step toward normalcy. They had to send their surviving children back to school. As Sandy Hook Elementary School was still a crime scene, an empty middle school in the nearby town of Monroe served as a replacement.

Crews of volunteers including movers, carpenters, and painters devoted themselves to the task of transforming Chalk Hill Middle School into Sandy Hook Elementary. They painted the walls to match Sandy Hook's walls. Teachers returned to classrooms outfitted with the furniture and equipment they had used at Sandy Hook. Students' desks and belongings were moved from the crime scene into their new classrooms at Chalk Hill, with every effort made to arrange things exactly as students had left them. The new school was renamed Sandy Hook Elementary, and even the sign in front of the school was the same one that had greeted Sandy

The community welcomed the Sandy Hook children back to school in January.

Hook students for years. It was all to make the transition easier for the children.

Back to School

On January 3, 2013, Sandy Hook students again crowded onto school buses. They saw streets decorated with green ribbons and signs broadcasting words of encouragement. A green-and-white banner welcomed them to a new Sandy Hook Elementary.

While eagerness to reunite with friends overshadowed most students' nervousness, many parents had a hard time letting go of fears for their

SNOWFLAKES FOR SANDY HOOK

As the new school was being readied for Sandy Hook students, the Connecticut Parent Teacher Association came up with an idea that would make the children's arrival more special. They asked people to send them handmade snowflakes to decorate the school.

Snowflakes soon began arriving—in envelopes and boxes, covered in glitter and beads and embroidery—from everywhere in the United States and countries all over the world.

The millions of snowflakes filled several rooms stacked floor to ceiling. Newtown residents were overwhelmed, and they couldn't help but be touched. There were more than enough to transform every school in town into a winter wonderland.

The snowflakes made the Sandy Hook students' return to school even more special. Each snowflake represented another person's love and willingness to reach out to a community in need.

children's safety. It helped that parents were allowed to accompany their children to school, making sure they were comfortable in their new surroundings. Parents and teachers were encouraged to get children back into normal routines at home and at school, and teachers focused on lessons and reconnecting with students. Counselors were on site to help students, teachers, and parents develop healthy ways of coping with their feelings after the shooting.

A task force was appointed to decide what to do with the building where the killings took place. Some people could not imagine bringing students back into the school after what had happened there. They recommended tearing down Sandy Hook Elementary and building a new school. Others felt strongly about renovating and reopening the existing school building. In May, the task force unanimously voted to tear down Sandy Hook and build a new school on its grounds. Construction was planned to be completed by January 2016.

There Is No Normal

Months after the shooting, home life was no closer to normal for the families of Newtown's victims. To help fill the holes in their lives, many parents strove to

RANDOM AND RARE

The relentlessness of media coverage and political debate following school shootings has a way of heightening the fear of these extremely rare events. In reality, such tragedies occur less than ten times a year and affect only a tiny fraction of students in the United States.[1] In fact, violence in general has dropped sharply in the United States—by approximately 50 percent— since the 1990s.[2]

find a larger meaning in the deaths of their children. Some found a purpose in political action, advocating for reforms that would make children and communities throughout the nation safer. Many established foundations in honor of their children devoted to a variety of causes, including violence prevention. The Hockleys honored their autistic son by creating the Dylan Hockley Memorial Fund. Donations would help other children with autism or special needs. Catherine Hubbard's parents planned to raise money to build an animal sanctuary in honor of their animal-loving daughter.

The child survivors of Sandy Hook were left to process very adult emotions after that traumatic day at school. Those who had lost siblings had to adjust to life without their playmates. Many struggled to understand why their sisters or brothers had been taken from them. Children who didn't lose siblings mourned their friends.

NEWTOWN

The healing process continues for Sandy Hook survivors.

Many Sandy Hook students began exhibiting symptoms of PTSD after the shooting. Some kids had nightmares. Others were easily startled by loud noises or were reluctant to go to school at all. Parents did their best to soothe their traumatized children's fears, and school faculty tried to minimize sights and sounds that would trigger memories of the shooting. But no one could erase the students' memories. The healing process was going to take a long, long time.

Investigation Continues

Intruding into the town's grief was an atmosphere of frustration surrounding the investigation. Aside from search warrant documents, officials had released little information even several months after the shooting. An official police report was not expected until as late as October 2013. Many in Newtown and elsewhere felt it was important to have more details, particularly about the shooter and what might have caused him to attack. They did not understand why the police refused to disclose information they felt might help make the community safer. Details about Lanza's journals and drawings—information that could shed light on his mental health—were still being withheld. "[Lanza's] mental state of mind is key here. Why is it that we can't talk about that?" Mark Barden implored.[3] Others took the search for answers into their own hands. Emilie Parker's parents arranged a

COLUMBINE SURVIVORS REACH OUT

In the aftermath of the shooting, families affected by the Columbine massacre expressed their condolences and offered words of wisdom to Sandy Hook families. They encouraged the families to grieve in their own way and to accept help when it was offered. And they offered a glimpse of what life might be like several years down the road in the healing process.

Rick Townsend, whose daughter died in the shooting at Columbine High School, said,

> Over time, the pain becomes less. Over time, although you'll never forget, never get over it, you can move on. And although it seems so distant now, you will feel joy again.[4]

meeting with Lanza's father. They did not reveal the details of their conversation, but it seemed the meeting brought them peace.

Adding to the frustration was the fact that some information was reportedly leaked to the press before the victims' families had been notified. A law enforcement official allegedly told the *New York Daily News* about a massive spreadsheet Lanza had used to meticulously collect data about other mass killings. Responding to reports of the leak, Lieutenant Vance said undisclosed details about the case had been discussed in a private law enforcement seminar. He expressed his disappointment that "someone in attendance chose not to . . . respect the families' right to know specifics of the investigation first."[5] Although the report was not confirmed, and the *New York Daily News* is known to sensationalize its reporting, it sparked demands for more details to be released to the public.

However, there were some details the Sandy Hook families never wanted revealed. They shuddered at the thought of images and video footage from the crime scene becoming viewable on the Internet. They did not want graphic images from the tragedy to be used to further political agendas or feed the imagination of the next copycat killer.

The families reached out to Connecticut lawmakers. They begged them to keep those painful images private, despite the public's right to know investigation details under the Freedom of Information Act (FOIA). State legislators passed a bill that would prevent graphic images or audio descriptions of the victims from being released. They argued the materials were exempt from the FOIA as they "could reasonably be expected to constitute an unwarranted invasion of personal privacy."[6] On June 5, 2013, Governor Malloy signed the law.

Love Wins

Perhaps the most important thing in helping the grief-stricken move forward was the love they felt from their community. The people of Newtown came together, reaching out to one another with hope and compassion. The president felt this compassion when he first arrived in Newtown. When he spoke at Newtown High School, he said, "As a community, you've inspired us, Newtown. In the face of indescribable violence . . . you've loved one another. This is how Newtown will be remembered."[7]

The Newtown community stands together as it continues healing.

And that is exactly how Newtown wanted to be remembered—for choosing love. In the days after the rampage, signs around town proclaimed, "We are Sandy Hook. We choose love."[8] Months later, Sandy Hook families and other Newtown residents were still determined that love would conquer the anger and sadness left by Adam Lanza. Newtown's love was the inspiration for first-grade victim Jesse Lewis's mother to establish the Jesse Lewis Choose Love Foundation. It was written in the words of the Sandy Hook Promise. And it was on Nelba Marquez-Greene's lips when she first spoke about that promise. "We are choosing love," she said. "In this way, we are honoring Ana's life, and the legacy of love and faith. Love wins. Love wins in Newtown, and may love win in America."[9]

TIMELINE

1992
Sandy Hook shooter Adam Lanza is born on April 22.

1998
The Lanza family settles in Newtown, Connecticut.

2010
Adam Lanza cuts off contact with everyone in his life except his mother.

2012
On December 14, Lanza shoots his way into Sandy Hook Elementary School and kills 20 students and six educators.

2012
On the evening of December 14, hundreds of mourners gather at candlelight vigils to honor the victims of the shooting.

2012

President Barack Obama speaks at an interfaith memorial service at Newtown High School on Sunday, December 16.

2012

On Monday, December 17, the first of the victims' funerals are held for Noah Pozner and Jack Pinto.

2012

Paul Simon sings "The Sound of Silence" at Victoria Soto's funeral, which hundreds of mourners attend on Wednesday, December 19.

2012

The last of the victims' funerals are held on December 22.

2012

Family members of victims collect mementos from the town's memorials on December 28 before they are cleared away.

TIMELINE

2013
On January 3, Sandy Hook students return to school.

2013
Sandy Hook parents and others organize a group called Sandy Hook Promise in January. The group's mission is to create change that will prevent future violence.

2013
President Obama calls for action on gun control in his State of the Union address on February 12.

2013
On April 4, Connecticut governor Dannel Malloy signs a bill implementing stricter gun control measures in the state, including banning assault weapons and high-capacity magazines.

2013

On April 8, families of victims accompany the president to Washington, DC, to lobby for national gun control legislation.

2013

On April 17, President Obama speaks about his determination to continue the fight for gun control after the US Senate fails to pass proposed amendments.

2013

On June 3, Obama hosts a national mental health conference at the White House. In his speech, he emphasizes erasing the stigma of mental illness.

2013

On June 5, Governor Malloy signs a bill preventing the release of graphic images and audio descriptions of shooting victims.

ESSENTIAL FACTS

Date of Event
December 14, 2012

Place of Event
Sandy Hook Elementary School in Newtown, Connecticut

Key Players
- Adam Lanza, the shooter

- Nancy Lanza, the shooter's mother

- The children: Charlotte Bacon, Daniel Barden, Olivia Engel, Josephine Gay, Dylan Hockley, Madeleine Hsu, Catherine Hubbard, Chase Kowalski, Jesse Lewis, Ana Marquez-Greene, James Mattioli, Grace McDonnell, Emilie Parker, Jack Pinto, Noah Pozner, Caroline Previdi, Jessica Rekos, Avielle Richman, Benjamin Wheeler, and Allison Wyatt

- The educators: Rachel D'Avino, Dawn Hochsprung, Anne Marie Murphy, Lauren Rousseau, Mary Sherlach, and Victoria Soto

- The families of the victims

- Dannel Malloy, the governor of Connecticut

- Barack Obama, the president of the United States

Highlights of Event

- On the morning of December 14, 2012, Adam Lanza fatally shot his mother. Then he drove to Sandy Hook Elementary School. He shot his way into the school and killed 20 children and six adults with a semiautomatic rifle. As police arrived, he took his own life.

- Close-knit Newtown inspired the nation with the love and support the community showed in the wake of tragedy. Residents held candlelight vigils and erected makeshift memorials for the victims of the shooting.

- The shooting spurred media coverage and heavy political debate. Conversations about gun control, mental health, and school safety increased dramatically. Many states passed new legislation in response to the tragedy.

Quote

"This is our first task, caring for our children. . . . That's how, as a society, we will be judged. And by that measure . . . can we honestly say that we're doing enough to keep our children, all of them, safe from harm? . . . If we're honest with ourselves, the answer's no. We're not doing enough. And we will have to change." —*President Barack Obama at the interfaith memorial service in Newtown*

GLOSSARY

arsenal
A collection of weapons.

assault
A physical attack on a person.

autism
A developmental disorder marked by impairments in social and communication skills.

barricade
To block access using a makeshift barrier.

condolence
An expression of sympathy.

homicidal
Intending to kill or capable of killing another person.

loophole
An ambiguity in a legal document that allows some to act against the intent of the document.

magazine
A part of a gun that holds cartridges full of ammunition.

massacre
The brutal murder of a large number of usually innocent people.

perpetrator
Someone who commits a crime.

predispose
To make someone more susceptible to something.

rampage
An episode in which someone attacks others publicly; it involves acts of violence against randomly selected victims.

semiautomatic
Able to fire repeatedly, with an additional depression of the trigger required for each shot.

trauma
An emotional shock caused by a terrifying or stressful event, often having long-term consequences.

triage
The sorting of patients based on their need for treatment.

ADDITIONAL RESOURCES

Selected Bibliography

Kalish, Rachel, and Michael Kimmel. "Suicide by Mass Murder: Masculinity, Aggrieved Entitlement, and Rampage School Shootings." *Health Sociology Review* 19.4 (2010): 451–464. Web. 7 June 2013.

Langman, Peter. *Why Kids Kill: Inside the Minds of School Shooters.* New York: Palgrave Macmillan, 2009. Print.

Raising Adam Lanza and Newtown Divided. Frank Koughan, writer and producer. *PBS.* WGBH Educational Foundation, 2013. Film.

Schildkraut, Jaclyn, and Glenn W. Muschert. (Forthcoming) "Violent Media, Guns, and Mental Illness: The Three Ring Circus of Causal Factors for School Massacres, as Related to Media Discourse." *Gun Violence and Public Life.* Ed. Ben Agger and Tim Luke. Boulder, CO: Paradigm. Print.

Further Readings

Agger, Ben, and Timothy W. Luke, eds. *There Is a Gunman on Campus: Tragedy and Terror at Virginia Tech.* Lanham, MD: Rowman and Littlefield, 2008. Print.

Gimpel, Diane Marczely. *The Columbine Shootings.* Minneapolis, MN: ABDO, 2012. Print.

Newman, Katherine S., et al. *Rampage: The Social Roots of School Shootings.* New York: Basic, 2005. Print.

Web Sites

To learn more about the Newtown school shooting, visit ABDO Publishing Company online at **www.abdopublishing.com**. Web sites about the Newtown school shooting are featured on our Book Links page. These links are routinely monitored and updated to provide the most current information available.

Places to Visit

Saint Rose Cemetery
Between Cherry Street and Black Cherry Lane in Newtown, Connecticut
203-426-5250
Several of the victims of the Sandy Hook shooting were laid to rest at Saint Rose Cemetery. Visitors there can pay their respects to Daniel Barden, Catherine Hubbard, and Jessica Rekos, among others.

The Sandy Ground: Where Angels Play
http://www.thesandygroundproject.org
With funding from the New Jersey Education Association and the New Jersey State Firefighters' Mutual Benevolent Association, the Sandy Ground Project is building 26 playgrounds across Connecticut, New Jersey, and New York to honor the 26 victims killed at Sandy Hook Elementary School.

SOURCE NOTES

Chapter 1. Lockdown

1. "Becky Virgalla, Newtown Shooting Survivor, Says Principal, Others Saved Her in Sandy Hook Rampage." *Huffington Post*. TheHuffingtonPost.com, 23 Dec. 2012. Web. 14 May 2013.

2. Kleinfield, N. R., Ray Rivera, and Serge F. Kovaleski. "Newtown Killer's Obsessions, in Chilling Detail." *New York Times*. New York Times, 28 Mar. 2013. Web. 20 May 2013.

3. "Becky Virgalla, Newtown Shooting Survivor, Says Principal, Others Saved Her in Sandy Hook Rampage." *Huffington Post*. TheHuffingtonPost.com, 23 Dec. 2012. Web. 14 May 2013.

4. "Building and Infrastructure Protection Series: Primer to Design Safe School Projects in Case of Terrorist Attacks and School Shootings." *Federal Emergency Management Agency*. US Department of Homeland Security, Jan. 2012. Web. 21 May 2013.

5. "Maryrose Kristopik, Sandy Hook Elementary School Shooting Hero, Hides Kids in Closet." *Huffington Post*. TheHuffingtonPost.com, 15 Dec. 2012. Web. 21 May 2013.

Chapter 2. A Quiet Boy

1. Alaine Griffin. "Raising Adam Lanza." *Hartford Courant*. Hartford Courant, 17 Feb. 2013. Web. 24 May 2013.

2. David M. Halbfinger. "A Gunman, Recalled as Intelligent and Shy, Who Left Few Footprints in Life." *New York Times*. New York Times, 14 Dec. 2012. Web. 28 May 2013.

3. Alaine Griffin. "Raising Adam Lanza." *Hartford Courant*. Hartford Courant, 17 Feb. 2013. Web. 24 May 2013.

4. Ibid.

Chapter 3. Newtown Changes Forever

1. N. R. Kleinfield, Ray Rivera, and Serge F. Kovaleski. "Newtown Killer's Obsessions, in Chilling Detail." *New York Times*. New York Times, 28 Mar. 2013. Web. 20 May 2013.

2. Susan Candiotti and Sarah Aarthun. "Police: 20 Children Among 26 Victims of Connecticut School Shooting." *CNN*. Cable News Network, 15 Dec. 2012. Web. 29 May 2013.

3. Ray Rivera. "Reliving Horror and Faint Hope at Massacre Site." *New York Times*. New York Times, 28 Jan. 2013. Web. 20 May 2013.

4. Ibid.

5. Ibid.

6. James Barron. "Nation Reels after Gunman Massacres 20 Children at School in Connecticut." *New York Times*. New York Times, 14 Dec. 2012. Web. 30 July 2013.

7. "Columbine High School Shootings." *Encyclopædia Britannica*. Encyclopædia Britannica, 2013. Web. 30 May 2013.

8. "Mass Shootings at Virginia Tech: Report of the Review Panel Presented to Governor Kaine, Commonwealth of Virginia." *Virginia Tech Review Panel*. Virginia.com, 16 Apr. 2007. Web. 30 July 2013.

9. Dan Frosch and Kirk Johnson. "Gunman Kills 12 in Colorado, Reviving Gun Debate." *New York Times*. New York Times, 20 July 2012. Web. 30 July 2013.

10. Ray Rivera. "Reliving Horror and Faint Hope at Massacre Site." *New York Times*. New York Times, 28 Jan. 2013. Web. 20 May 2013.

Chapter 4. The Truth Sinks In

1. "A Parent's Worst Nightmare: Looking for a Child among the Survivors of the Sandy Hook Elementary School Shooting." *CBS New York*. CBS Local Media, 17 Dec. 2012. Web. 31 May 2013.

2. David Ariosto and Thom Patterson. "Comforting Survivors." *CNN*. Cable News Network, 15 Dec. 2012. Web. 1 June 2013.

3. "A Parent's Worst Nightmare: Looking for a Child among the Survivors of the Sandy Hook Elementary School Shooting." *CBS New York*. CBS Local Media, 17 Dec. 2012. Web. 31 May 2013.

4. Peter Applebome and Michael Wilson. "'Who Would Do This to Our Poor Little Babies.'" *New York Times*. New York Times, 14 Dec. 2012. Web. 31 May 2013.

5. "Newtown Police Chief Shares His Story." *CBS News*. CBS Interactive, 22 Dec. 2012. Web. 29 May 2013.

6. "President Obama Makes a Statement on the Shooting in Newtown, Connecticut." *White House*. US Government, 14 Dec. 2012. Web. 6 June 2013.

7. Ibid.

8. J. Schildkraut and G. W. Muschert. "Media Salience and the Framing of Mass Murder in Schools: A Comparison of the Columbine and Sandy Hook Massacres." 2013. Manuscript submitted for publication (copy on file with author).

9. Doug Stanglin. "ID Mixup of Shooter Prompts Facebook Plea: 'It Wasn't Me.'" *USA Today*. USA Today, 15 Dec. 2012. Web. 30 July 2013.

10. "Malloy Speaks Newtown School Shooting 6:00 p.m." *YouTube*. YouTube, 14 Dec. 2012. Web. 3 June 2013.

SOURCE NOTES CONTINUED

Chapter 5. Grief and Remembrance

1. Kelly Conniff. "Family Photos: Obama Meets with Relatives of Newtown Victims." *Time*. Time, 17 Dec. 2012. Web. 5 June 2013.

2. Susan Candiotti and Greg Botelho. "Obama to Town Wracked by School Shooting: 'These Tragedies Must End.'" *CNN*. Cable News Network, 16 Dec. 2012. Web. 5 June 2013.

3. Bill Chappell. "Obama: 'We Have Wept with You.'" *NPR*. NPR, 16 Dec. 2012. Web. 5 June 2013.

4. Ibid.

5. "Transcript: President Obama at Sandy Hook Prayer Vigil." *NPR*. NPR, 16 Dec. 2012. Web. 5 June 2013.

6. Ibid.

7. Andy Newman. "Dec. 16 Updates on Connecticut Shooting Aftermath." *The Lede*. New York Times, 16 Dec. 2012. Web. 5 June 2013.

8. Ibid.

9. "Final Funerals for Newtown Shooting Victims." *CBS News*. CBS Interactive, 22 Dec. 2012. Web. 5 June 2013.

Chapter 6. Seeking Answers

1. Matthew Lysiak and Bill Hutchinson. "Emails Show History of Illness in Lanza's Family, Mother Had Worries about Gruesome Images." *New York Daily News*. NYDailyNews.com, 8 Apr. 2013. Web. 7 June 2013.

2. Alaine Griffin. "Raising Adam Lanza." *Hartford Courant*. Hartford Courant, 17 Feb. 2013. Web. 24 May 2013.

3. Peter Langman, PhD. *Why Kids Kill: Inside the Minds of School Shooters*. New York: Palgrave MacMillan, 2009. Print. 8.

4. "Seung Hui Cho's 'Manifesto.'" *SchoolShooters.info*. Peter Langman, 2012. Web. 7 June 2013.

Chapter 7. Taking Action

1. Jaclyn Schildkraut and Tiffany Cox Hernandez. "Laws that Bit the Bullet: A Review of Legislative Responses to School Shootings." *American Journal of Criminal Justice*. Southern Criminal Justice Association, 25 May 2013. PDF.

2. "The Sandy Hook Promise." *Sandy Hook Promise*. Sandy Hook Promise, n.d. Web. 10 June 2013.

3. Saki Knafo. "Connecticut Task Force on Gun Violence Holds Hearing at Newtown High School." *Huffington Post*. TheHuffingtonPost.com, 30 Jan. 2013. Web. 10 June 2013.

4. Colleen Curtis. "Weekly Address: Sandy Hook Victim's Mother Calls for Commonsense Gun Responsibility Reforms." *White House Blog*. US Government, 13 Apr. 2013. Web. 11 June 2013.

5. Ibid.

6. David Ariosto. "Sandy Hook Hearing Reveals Sharp Divide on Gun Control." *CNN.* Cable News Network, 29 Jan. 2013. Web. 10 June 2013.

7. Peter Applebome and Jonathan Weisman. "Obama Invokes Newtown Dead in Pressing for New Gun Laws." *New York Times.* New York Times, 8 Apr. 2013. Web. 10 June 2013.

8. Ibid.

9. Terence Burlij and Christina Bellantoni. "Gun Control Advocates Lose 'Round One.'" *PBS NewsHour.* MacNeil/Lehrer Productions, 18 Apr. 2013. Web. 30 July 2013.

10. Liza Long. "I Am Adam Lanza's Mother." *The Blue Review.* Boise State University, 15 Dec. 2012. Web. 10 June 2013.

11. "Obama Says 'No Shame' in Seeking Mental Health Treatment." *Washington Post.* Washington Post, 3 June 2013. Web. 10 June 2013.

Chapter 8. Moving Forward

1. J. Schildkraut. "Media and Massacre: A Comparative Analysis of the Reporting of the 2007 Virginia Tech Shootings." *Fast Capitalism* 9.1 (2012). Web. 30 July 2013.

2. Bill Dedman. "10 Myths about School Shootings." *NBC News.* NBCUniversal, 10 Oct. 2007. Web. 12 June 2013.

3. Ray Rivera. "Lawmakers and Relatives Want More Information Released about Newtown Gunman." *New York Times.* New York Times, 29 Mar. 2013. Web. 12 June 2013.

4. "Columbine Survivors Tell Newtown Families 'Over Time, Pain Lessens.'" *Denver Post.* Denver Post, 22 Dec. 2012. Web. 12 June 2013.

5. Davis Dunavin. "Report: Sandy Hook School Shooter Conducted Years of Research." *Newtown Patch.* Patch, 18 Mar. 2013. Web. 12 June 2013.

6. "Freedom of Information Act Exemptions." *U.S. Securities and Exchange Commission.* US Securities and Exchange Commission, 1 Dec. 1999. Web. 12 June 2013.

7. "Transcript: President Obama at Sandy Hook Prayer Vigil." *NPR.* NPR, 16 Dec. 2012. Web. 5 June 2013.

8. Shannon Hicks. "'We Are Sandy Hook We Choose Love' a Conscious, Defiant Choice Inspired by MLK." *Newtown Bee.* Newtown Bee, 8 Feb. 2013. Web. 12 June 2013.

9. Jeff Cohen. "Families of Newtown Victims Launch New Initiative." *NPR.* NPR, 14 Jan. 2013. Web. 12 June 2013.

INDEX

ABOUT THE AUTHOR

Lisa Owings has a degree in English and creative writing from the University of Minnesota. She has written and edited a wide variety of educational books for young people. Lisa lives in Andover, Minnesota, with her husband.

ABOUT THE CONSULTANT

Jaclyn Schildkraut is a doctoral candidate in the School of Criminal Justice at Texas State University. Her research interests include school shootings, homicide trends, mediatization effects, and crime theories. She has published in *Homicide Studies*, the *American Journal of Criminal Justice,* and *Criminal Justice Studies*.